CW00552979

THE SEDUCER'S COOKBOOK

JAMES CHATTO

cartoons by ffolkes

DAVID & CHARLES
Newton Abbot London North Pomfret (Vt)

British Library Cataloguing in Publication Data

Chatto, James
The Seducer's Cookbook.
1. Cookery
I. Title
641.5 TX717
ISBN 0-7153-8201-2

Typeset by ABM Typographics Ltd., Hull and printed in Great Britain by A. Wheaton & Co. Ltd., Exeter for David & Charles (Publishers) Limited Brunel House Newton Abbot Devon

Published in the United States of America by David & Charles Inc
North Pomfret Vermont 05053 USA

Contents

Conversion Tables

Oven temperatures

Gas Mark			
Gas Mark	½	250°F	120°C
	1	275°F	140°C
	2	300°F	150°C
	3	325°F	170°C
	4	350°F	180°C
	5	375°F	190°C
	6	400°F	200°C
	7	425°F	220°C
	8	450°F	230°C
	9	475°F	240°C

Liquid measures

(approximate conversions)

1pt (20fl oz)	570ml
½pt (10fl oz)	275
¼pt (5fl oz)	150
1 mug (8fl oz)	250
1 cup (6fl oz)	168
1 level tablespoon (1fl oz)	25
1 level dessertspoon (½fl oz)	12
1 level teaspoon (1/6fl oz)	5

Dry weights

(approximate conversions)

1lb (16oz)	450g
½lb (8oz)	225
¼lb (4oz)	110
1oz	25
1 mug (8oz)	225
1 cup flour (5oz)	125
1 cup rice (6oz)	175
1 tablespoon (1oz)	25
1 dessertspoon (⅔oz)	18
1 teaspoon (⅓oz)	9

General Principles

The keynote of the classic seduction has always been disguise. Zeus, the authority of his day, seems to have used no other tactic, and Don Juan had considerable success in a seraglio by dressing up as a girl. Unfortunately though, much of the old expertise has been lost. No one these days can change themselves into a shower of gold and impersonating a bull leads only to ribald laughter and possible arrest. Even the occasions when a trenchcoat, a cigarette and a snarl will win a heart have become increasingly rare.

The principles of romance, however, remain the same. You are aiming to fulfil the lady's fantasy, defined or still unconscious, to resemble the man of her dreams, for her image of the ideal lover will seduce her far more effectively than yours. Catering to this you will flatter and entertain and probably, at last, fascinate. At any rate you will have made friends, and friendship does not always bar romance. People adore having trouble taken on their behalf and undivided attention is refreshing as an alternative to fashionable cool.

There are many advantages to eating at home. In a room of your own no waiters hover to interrupt or insult, there is no Day of Judgement when the bill arrives and no chance of your guest spotting a friend or ex-husband at another table. The tortuous drive back through city traffic can be forgotten, the sobering effect of cold night air ignored, and you can plan the menu and create an atmosphere for the exclusive pleasure of your intended.

The major problem is diagnosing her particular dream. Is she hungry to be pampered? Does she relish confrontation? Is her secret need a man who, in the privacy of his flat, wears a kimono and speaks only Dutch? There are ways of finding out.

Let us assume that, standing by the crisp-bowl at a party, you suddenly catch sight of Helen of Troy, surrounded by a gaggle of unworthy men, bored by their braggadocio. Instead of joining the fan club, instruct a friend, trusted or better still gay, to infiltrate himself into the conversation. Stand within earshot as he pesters her about her job, likes and dislikes, old boyfriends etcetera, and search her words for clues. As her attention flags and she is looking around for escape your friend introduces you. Here insouciance can work: gaze and smile quietly then leave without betraying anything of yourself. Engineer one further brief encounter and be sure to discover her name and address from your host before going home. Once there, pen a discreet dinner invitation and deliver it by hand so she receives it the very next morning, describing yourself as someone she met last night. The host, well primed with promises of reciprocation, will inform her, should she ask, that you are a man of mystery, exceptionally talented and kind, but that no one knows you well. With luck, curiosity will prompt her to accept the challenge.

Now is the time to consolidate your information. Indulge in further research if you can do it quietly, be objective about your physique and acting abilities, and decide at last what sort of person she would most like to have dinner with. You could be disastrously wrong: she may see through your disguise, realise at some point during the soup that you are not in fact a streetwise kid from the Bronx or a genuine gondolier, but at least she will know that you have tried. If she points and howls with laughter do not crumble: next to food, humour is the finest heat-source in the world for melting ice.

* * *

Sweeping people off their feet demands an uninterrupted stroke of the broom. Hours spent in the kitchen, like mirrors in the hall, offer your guest dangerous moments of reflection, so nearly all the recipes in this book are designed to be prepared well in advance, and written with the sort of cook in mind who is uncertain where in his flat the kitchen is. Its location is the first step towards a successful evening, then, once inside, assess the capabilities of your equipment, lay out all the ingredients you need, pre-heat the oven and set to work.

A few general rules might help the inexperienced: first of all, always cook when you are hungry. This turns the preparation of food into a pleasure, stimulates the imagination and reminds you to taste the meal as you go along. Wear rubber gloves when dealing with garlic, onions and raw fish as their personalities linger through many baths, competing with your own charisma. The smell of frying is another nomadic aroma, exploring distant chambers, so cook with a window open and the door shut. Have all changes of plates and cutlery laid out somewhere ready to use half an hour before your guest arrives and wash up as you cook.

The atmosphere you desire should not be restricted to the room in which you are eating, so give some thought to the decoration and lighting throughout your apartment. Bedsitters are at an advantage here with only one area to adapt, but there is nothing to stop others setting up a table in the bedroom and entertaining there.

Wherever you decide on, heat the home until you are comfortable in any room in shirtsleeves and bare feet, and clean thoroughly, especially in the bathroom, for however rugged you may wish to appear, dirt will always be a turn-off.

As regards planning a menu, make a list of the dishes and ingredients you need, but be prepared to change your mind in the marketplace if the chicken looks dry but the lamb good. Aim for four or five courses of little amounts. This means more work, but there are advantages. It may be that she will sit down to eat with the remark that she is allergic to spinach; if you have hung your hopes on just one dish, an exquisite minaret of the iron-packed chenopodiac, you could be in trouble, though luck like that looks suspiciously like a general veto from the Fates. Many courses are also more exciting, extend the time before any traumatic physical overtures begin, and help to prevent overeating if you are nervous. Try not to get drunk, eat at the same speed as your guest and hide toothbrush and paste in the kitchen for a surreptitious clean while you are getting the coffee.

Finally, and most importantly, enjoy yourself. In seduction as in poker, whether you hold a straight or a pair of queens, the satisfaction may lie in getting your hands on the pot but the beauty is all in the shimmering aesthetic of the game.

Getting the Pagan Right

A retentive memory is one of the seducer's most valuable assets, as useful as a flair for gumshoe cunning. Picture him in a library, for example, where his wicked eye alights upon his intended. She is reading a well-thumbed copy of Byron, her eyes wide as she lives through Don Juan's affair with Haidée on 'one of the wild and smaller Cyclades'. He does not attract her attention, doesn't even stare, but when she has gone, bribes the librarian for her name and taste in books. A month later he is sitting over a tepid espresso in a café when the lady walks in with a friend. If he can recall her name, he could be in business. He listens to their conversation. His beloved, it transpires, is bored with England, tired of Englishmen and of dreary English restaurants. Her dreams are troubled by visions of pagan supermen from the *Iliad,* dancing on a beach.

Put yourself in the seducer's place. It could be that this is not the sort of person you would choose to have in your house, but perhaps she is rich and beautiful or in a position to offer you a job. Send her an invitation to dinner laced with quotations from Homer and sign it Diomedes.

The atmosphere of the evening must from the outset be one of thinly veiled savagery. You are aiming here for the electric tension of naked animal desires seething under a veneer of civilisation. Have a bath and think for a few minutes of your home on the sun-swept island of Machismos: the yellow hills where goats crop the wild sage, the olive tree that you love like a mother, the deserted beach where you pull your boat up, and the sea itself, translucent and motionless in the heat. Most evenings there you walk up into the village to sit with the men, greet them with a grunt and drink yourself into a fight; tonight, however, you have invited the English lady back to supper.

This sort of mental preparation is most important. An actor friend of mine who found it difficult to sustain his imagination would, having pictured the scene, find a word that he could use, like a hypnotist, to conjure back the atmosphere. I would suggest something in gibberish full of bitterness and lone-wolf desire. This done, get dressed. The ideal costume must be plimsolls, old but white and worn without socks, white jeans, again clean but not new, and a dark blue crew-neck sweater with the sleeves half pulled up. Do not shave. Prowl into the kitchen. The walk is important: body straight, head slightly bowed, a little frown;

enjoy the suppleness of the tennis shoes and think of a hunting animal. If you can't manage this, forget it: it has to be dead right or it will appear ridiculous. Practise smiling. This must be unexpected and rare, revealing a flash of white teeth, if possible, and a sudden glimpse of boyishness. It is the old fantasy of sheik and maiden, Tarzan and Jane; let her see through your savagery to the innocence.

Back on Machismos your place was a little stone cell with a rough wood table, two chairs, a truckle bed and a shelf; short of major redecoration this is difficult to achieve. The best you can do is to think simple. Imagine that you have borrowed the place from a friend and are living as best you can in a strange environment. Put all the books away, hide the television and remove any banal objects to the side of the room. Use your own judgement and resources for props: a much handled hunting knife perhaps, left idly in an obtrusive position.

An open fire is far and away the best lighting for any seduction, but if you do not have one, make do with a candle: it is less obvious than a hurricane lamp from your fishing boat and draws the attention into the middle of the room, but do not light it at once. To lead her into a candlelit room, or worse, to usher her into one, is to put her on her guard. Light it casually after about half an hour. By the end of the evening you should be left with just this one source of illumination, but switching off table lamps is a little crude. Instead prepare other candles by cutting them down to about an inch and when she is out of the room for a moment light them, placing two in the area of each extinguished lamp. After half an hour they will surreptitiously go out and the effect you seek will have been achieved with no apparent intervention.

Music plays a bizarre part in your life on Machismos. There are the dark Zorban times when it can take possession of your soul, but those are occasions when you are amongst men. It is like the sea to you, very personal and not part of your dealings with the opposite sex. Besides, this is not an evening to be spent at the gramophone, handling records. A long tape would be better, but not bouzouki music: Greek sounds have become so instantly recognisable. Much better are the sort of ballads found on a record of soft French rock, discs with a growling man mumbling in a foreign language, all of a rhythm. Play them very quietly lest they intrude on the long silences to come when you are both sitting on the floor, yards apart, simmering.

Some tough guys eschew cooking, but not this character. On Machismos, alone, you learned to fend for yourself, grateful for the marvellous bounty of the sea, the pasture and the mountainside. Olive oil was free, and wild sage, rigani and rosemary grew in abundance about your doorstep. There you ate one meal a day, meat or fish, stewed in an outdoor oven with garlic, and in the evening with your beer and ouzo devoured souvlaki and nibbled at mezethes.

Away from all that, you choose to stay loyal to your native cuisine and tonight for her you have thrown together, quite casually, a feast representative of your real life, to honour the lady. Share with her your reverence for the fruits of earth and sea.

Beer and ouzo are your natural beverages, but tonight you offer wine, bottles of Domestica with the labels all soaked off, and afterwards you could bring out a half-full bottle of Metaxa Greek brandy and two cheap and stemless liqueur glasses, as simple as your honest soul.

Remember your rugged mantra and let her talk, staring intently as if puzzled by the new emotions this goddess is awakening in you. Relax with your body but burn behind the eyes.

MENU

Taramasalata

Souvlaki
Chicken Livers
Ram's Testicles

Vegetable Moussaka
Psario Bianco
Baked Mullet
Woman's Thigh Rissoles
Fassoli Kai Krea

Fresh Fruit

Greek Coffee, Brandy

Obligatory is a dish of sliced tomatoes with oil, lemon juice and oregano, and another of feta cheese, served with the main course. A method for making Greek coffee appears on p. 60.

Taramasalata

Making taramasalata properly takes a fair amount of time and the results are sometimes dubious. It might be better to buy some from a shop and pretend it's yours by spooning it into a bowl, tasting it, and adding 1 tbsp lemon juice if it's too salty or 1 tbsp cream if it's too sharp. Either way, drop 1 tbsp olive oil onto the top and eat it with fresh bread in your

fingers. Grunt out the information that you prefer to make it with the pressed roe of grey mullet not cod's roe.
If, however, you wish to make a taramasalata, here is one way.

¼lb smoked cod's roe
¼ tsp powdered garlic
1 spring onion, chopped
1 slice white bread
3 tbsp olive oil
juice of ½ lemon
black pepper
1 tbsp milk

Use slightly stale bread and cut off its crusts. Crumble it very finely into the milk. Now put the onion and oil into a blender and liquidise. Add the breadcrumbs, garlic, lemon juice and a little pepper, and blend again. Scoop the cod's roe out of its skin and mix it with the rest with a fork. Add more pepper to taste. Let it stand for 3 hours, outside the fridge.

Souvlaki

The only disadvantage with souvlaki is that they have to be cooked on the spot. Your guest, left alone, may remember the last time she saw you, coming out of the chemist with a scarf and macintosh, snivelling with flu. One solution is to enlist the help of a friend and secrete him in the kitchen to cook them, silently and without personal appearance. Make him leave immediately his job is done, distracting her attention from the noise of the front door with a plangent anecdote.

4 lamb chops or pork chops
juice of two lemons
¼pt *olive* oil
1 tsp oregano
1 tsp basil
2 tsp coarse black pepper
salt
fresh white bread

Cut meat into ¾in cubes. Soak in a marinade of lemon juice, oil, herbs and seasoning for 4-5 hours. Thread the meat onto souvlaki sticks (9in bamboo spears). Heat grill to maximum and broil the sticks, turning occasionally, until the outside is slightly charred. Dip each stick back in the marinade and serve with fresh white bread, pulling the meat from the skewers with your teeth. Supply napkins.

Chicken Livers

½lb chicken livers
1 tbsp butter
salt and pepper
1 tbsp flour
2 tsp oregano
1 lemon

Roll each liver in the flour and fry briefly in the oil, salt, pepper and oregano until they are brown. Squeeze the lemon over them and eat at once.

Ram's Testicles

Hard to come by without a fight since most rams are used for breeding. Only your own unimpeachable honesty, however, will forbid you to use lamb's kidneys and swear that they are the real McCoy.

½lb ram's testicles
1 egg, beaten
2 tsp sage
juice of 1 lemon
3 tbsp olive oil
3 tbsp flour
salt and pepper

Cut the testicles in half (if kidneys, skin and take out the core of veins), dip them in the egg, then the flour and fry with the sage in the oil, sprinkling with salt and pepper, until they are tender. Serve with a sauce made from the frying juices and the juice of 1 lemon.

Vegetable Moussaka

2 aubergines
2 large potatoes
2 medium-sized onions
1 green pepper
½lb carrots
½lb tomatoes
½lb courgettes
½ cup olive oil
½ tsp nutmeg
2 tsp fresh parsley
2 tsp basil
1 tsp powdered garlic
½ tsp ground caraway seed
salt and pepper

Slice aubergines and soak in salt water for 1 hour. Chop onions, peppers and carrots and fry lightly in the oil. Slice potatoes thinly and boil in salt water until soft. Add the aubergines and boil them for 5 minutes more. Peel and chop tomatoes and chop courgettes. Add these with all the herbs and spices to the frying vegetables and simmer for 5 minutes. Remove from heat. Drain potatoes and aubergines and lay them evenly on the other vegetables. Cover with this sauce, based on a béchamel:

1½ tbsp butter
2 rounded tbsp flour
1pt milk
2 eggs, separated
1 bay leaf
½ tsp nutmeg
2 tbsp grated parmesan
salt and pepper

Melt butter and blend in flour. Dribble in the milk and stir until all is smooth. Beat egg yolks and stir them in with the bay leaf, nutmeg and salt and pepper. Beat egg whites into foam and when the sauce is beginning to thicken, fold them in, with the parmesan. Pour over the vegetables to cover them about 1in deep. Bake for 1 hour in an oven at 150°C (300°F) Mark 2.

Psario Bianco

Back just after dawn with a boat full of fish. You sell the fat mullet and stew a selection of the smaller ones for yourself.

1 medium-sized onion, chopped
1 tbsp butter
1 tbsp olive oil
½ heaped tbsp cornflour
1pt white stock
2 medium-sized potatoes, peeled, chopped
salt and pepper
1 small grey mullet
2 red snappers
1 small sole
6 large scampi, shelled
2 tsp oregano
¼pt milk
1 tsp paprika

Ask the fishmonger to clean the fish and scale them but keep the heads. Cut off the tails and fins. On Machismos you ate the heads; elsewhere they can startle a diner, but include them if you wish to be really ethnic. Fry the onion in butter and oil until soft. Smooth in flour and then milk. Add all the other ingredients and simmer for 1 hour. If you like, remove the fish and take out all the bones, a long but worthwhile activity. Simmer when you reheat it for a further 30 minutes. Serve with a tomato salad, made from the fruit, olive oil and lemon juice, salt, pepper and sage, and offer fresh white bread. A plate of washed feta cheese is marvellous with it.

Baked Mullet

Easy but glamorous, and physical to eat because of the bones.

1 large grey mullet (1½lb or 2lb)
1 tbsp butter
1 tsp oregano
1 tbsp wholewheat flour
1 tsp sage
salt and pepper
4 cloves garlic

Have the fishmonger clean the fish. Once home, wash it, cut out the fins along the back and scrape off any forgotten scales. Lay it on its back in a baking tin. Rub salt and butter over the inside of the fish. Crush the garlic cloves and place them inside with the other herbs. Sprinkle the flour over the outside of the fish and bake it in an oven at 200°C (400°F) Mark 6 for 30-40 minutes, depending on the size. Beside the fish in the tin lay 3 or 4 tomatoes, finger-sized pieces of parsnip, whole mushrooms and serve with rice.

Woman's Thigh Rissoles

So-called because of their smooth texture, these rissoles slip occasionally into northeastern Greek cookery from across the Turkish border.

5oz minced beef or lamb
1 medium-sized onion, chopped fine
3 tbsp cooked rice
2oz cheese, grated
small saucer of flour
2 eggs, beaten
½ tsp ground cummin
1 tsp salt
1 tsp black pepper
1 tsp Worcestershire sauce
1 tbsp olive oil

Fry the onion in the oil until it is brown. Mix it with meat, rice, cheese, half the egg, cummin, salt and pepper until it is very smooth. Mould into four balls and roll them in the flour, flattening them slightly, then grill until dark on the outside. Mix Worcestershire sauce with the remaining egg and fry it like an omelette in a dry pan. Serve on hot plates with the egg draped over the rissoles and pieces of lemon and tomato.

Fassoli Kai Krea

Leg knuckle of lamb
½lb broad beans
2 medium-sized onions
4 tomatoes
3 tbsp tomato ketchup
1 tbsp butter
salt and pepper
2 tsp Worcestershire sauce
2 tsp oregano
2 tsp basil
1 tsp thyme
½ tsp nutmeg
¼lb mushrooms

Soak beans in salted water overnight or use the tinned variety. Chop the onions and fry them in a large, heavy casserole until they are soft. Skin tomatoes, chop and throw them in. Simmer for 3 minutes then take off the heat. Stir in the ketchup and Worcestershire sauce. Rub joint with salt and oregano, lay it on top of the onions and sprinkle the other herbs around it. Bake, uncovered, in the oven at 150°C (300°F) Mark 2 for 1 hour, then take out the meat. Mix the beans and mushrooms with the stew, replace the meat and bake for another hour. Do not baste or stir any more. The surface may appear overcooked: relax and serve it with a cool green salad.

Rève Gauche

The true Bohemian, mystical, tubercular, self-obsessed and possessed of genius, is rarely seen to eat, except where he can scrounge a meal off the wife of a café proprietor. He is supposed to spend the few pence he makes from his sketches or parental pension on materials. As a romantic he cares deeply for the individual, a passion that manifests itself in concern for the poor he has never met and for himself, but all these rules are broken by the arrival upon the scene of love.

In reality, perhaps, a Bohemian's true mistress is his own talent or a dimly realised angel he refers to as his aesthetic; women are merely models or hot-water bottles or excuses for self-expression. To emulate the Bohemian, therefore, for the purposes of seduction, it is necessary to set aside this principle of his existence and concentrate on the more extraneous mumbo-jumbo of the left bank.

Who will be taken in by this facade? The Bohemienne herself for one, but it is unadvisable to compete. It is an intensely jealous demi-monde, from the scruffiness of the clothes to the philosophical stance. More susceptible might be the bored heiress or the young lady about to embark upon a lifestyle and seeking guidance.

Choose your medium—writer, painter, sculptor or composer—from the area of greatest innocence on the lady's part. Oscar Wilde used to keep a half-finished oil-painting on an easel in his rooms at Oxford, but if you learn that your intended is a devotee of galleries, substitute untidy piles of scrawled manuscript paper with a title on the top like 'Verlustegefrau, A Symphonic Poem for Contralto and Percussion'. If she asks you what it is about, say it is about her.

Advantages and pitfalls stalk arm-in-arm along the highway of this idiom. For a start, it is usual to be dismissive of all others working in your field and humbly ignorant of all other fields. This is clearly useful as it conceals stupidity but can lead to an impression of insufferable smugness, so try and imbue your answers to her provocations with a deep humanity, rare in one so precociously gifted. Take a few works that you do know, as unlikely or bizarre as possible, and elevate them to masterpieces in your conversation—Vian rather than Sartre, Braque above Picasso.

As regards your flat, think garret. Drape furniture with ancient lengths of velvet, cover carpets with tatty rugs and denude the hall or corridor of lampshades to give the im-

pression that you have only the one room. The environment should reflect your independence from the past, exciting though it was to have been brought up by whores in Paris or Karakas only to learn that your father was an Irish peer or even the finest swordsman in all France. Your heritage from him is exquisite taste and, if you feel you have to imply a good body, a forsaken career as an Olympic fencer. One or two heirlooms are permissible on the periphery of the candlelight, a lump of white marble or a beat-up samovar perhaps, but mask the hi-fi behind more old cloth, erasing all signs of opulence.

To go the whole way, study Wallis's *Death of Chatterton* and strip the room of all but the barest essentials, tear up some poems and scatter them by the bed, leave empty phials of laudanum everywhere.

Your approach to the lady can be two-pronged, and both prongs are to be observed in Shaw's *Candida.* Reading it through with yourself as Marchbanks you will see that women look upon the Bohemian as someone to mother or as an angel of unconventional romance, bearing her away on the steed of his youthful genius. In the first case all will be forgiven, in the second you might have to work a little harder: learn by heart ten lines of Shakespeare (one line is commonplace, two pretentious, ten unusual) and introduce them casually late into the evening. Lay a yellow rose between her cutlery.

As you lie in the bath, the cooking done, work out whether you are a Bohemian through need or by conscious choice. If it's by choice then be aware that your books make you a fortune in South America or that 'Verlustegefrau' is being used as the soundtrack to a black-and-white Czech expressionist film. If, on the other hand, poverty dictates your surroundings, arm yourself with an indifference to personal suffering and a concern for humanity which none the less avoids both bitterness and politics. Pretend you have travelled everywhere or nowhere, apologise for nothing.

These days the Punk and the New Romantics can be heard referring to themselves as Bohemians. While it is true that they possess enough narcissism to qualify, they are disciples rather than creators except in the limited art form of dandyism, and even then real achievement is haphazard. More traditional wear might be a soft billowy shirt, old black velvet trousers and black boots, with the subtlest touch of dark eye make-up, an effect that is always intriguing. Unlike the Greek evening, candles can be lit before she arrives as they are anyway your natural lighting. Offer wine from a jug and invest in some good coffee. The music of the Bohemian quarter is usually live and impromptu—whores and apaches melting into complex choreography, Mario Lanza coaxed into an aria in a humble bar, the scruffy guy in the corner turning out to be Woody Guthrie. In your apartment, unless you can hire a friend to serenade on a saxophone, blues dripping down the tenement fire-escapes, play any kind of solo music, Chopin or Joe Pass or lute music. Orchestras tend to sound luxurious.

Words are your allies tonight, but beware of talking too much and of pontificating. Discover her pet subject and beg to learn more about it; a lady who has opened her heart to you is more likely to open her arms.

MENU

Bullshot Soup

Palette of Crudités
Artichokes
Tongue in Cheeks

Risotto
Couscous
Liver and Bacon
Hamburger Esterhazy and Kraut
Ratatouille

Drunken Peaches
Lemon Sorbet

Coffee

If you decide on a ratatouille for the main course start with something other than artichokes.

Bullshot Soup

A fiendish concoction, powerful enough to render the rest of the meal redundant, either because it has worked or because you find yourself suddenly alone.

2 cans consomme
1/3pt vodka
1 tomato juice mixer
1 tbsp Worcestershire sauce

Mix it all together, seasoning if you wish, and serve it from a tureen.

Palette of Crudités

An unusual way to encounter dips. Three large carrots, celery and any other of the vegetables mentioned for Nam Prik Pak (p.27) are washed and cut into pieces the size of your finger. Then, on a spotless, wooden, artist's palette, dollop dips of different colours like paint. Beside them, offer a small bowl of salad dressing as if it were linseed oil.

Green dip:
1 ripe avocado pear
2 tbsp mayonnaise
1/2 tsp grated nutmeg
salt and pepper

Mash the avocado with the other ingredients.

Ochre dip:
1 small tub cream cheese
1 tsp French mustard
salt and pepper
1 tbsp grated parmesan
1/2 tsp turmeric

Blend everything thoroughly with a fork.

Pink dip:
See the recipe for taramasalata on p.10.

Artichokes

A wonderful adventure to eat that gets better and better until the treasure of the heart of the choke. Cut the stalks off the artichokes right up beyond the southernmost leaves. Soak them in salted water for 30 minutes. Boil them in different salted water for 20 minutes and serve with a jugful of melted butter, lots of salt and pepper, and a bowl in the middle for tooth-scraped leaves. Remember to supply a fork for eating the tender heart.

Tongue in Cheeks

An entertaining way of using up old French mustard.

4 small leeks
4 thin slices tongue or smoked ham
2 tsp French mustard
1½ tbsp butter
1 heaped tbsp plain flour
⅓pt milk
½ tsp paprika
½ tsp nutmeg
salt and pepper
¼lb strong cheddar cheese

Clean and trim the leeks. Boil them in salted water for 3 minutes. Smear ½ tsp mustard on each slice of tongue and sprinkle lightly with salt. Roll each slice around a leek and pack them flat in an ovenproof dish. Make a sauce by melting the butter and beating the flour, nutmeg and paprika into a paste with it. Dribble in the milk, stirring constantly, until it is smooth. As it begins to thicken add salt and pepper to taste, then tip in the cheese. Pour it immediately over the leeks and bake for 45 minutes in an oven at 200°C (400°F) Mark 6.

Risotto

Gork is a Canadian term that covers any melange from ratatouille to chilli. It forms the basis of most garret meals and has its own precise beginnings: two onions chopped and fried with salt, pepper and herbs. A usual but not obligatory next step is the addition of tomatoes which, after stewing for 5 minutes, results in the simplest gork which can be added to any staple like rice, spaghetti or beans, unadorned. It is common, however, to go on to activate the gork with other ingredients, creating personal Frankensteins with meat or other vegetables.
Put on an album of early blues and fry.

2 medium-sized onions, chopped
1 tsp oregano
1 tsp marjoram
2 peeled tomatoes
4 rashers streaky bacon
¼lb mushrooms and/or green pepper
2 tbsp vinegar
salt and black pepper
1 tsp castor sugar
1pt mug dry patna rice
1 tbsp Dijon mustard
½pt chicken stock
2oz grated strong cheddar
2 tsp grated parmesan
1 tsp nutmeg
2 tbsp oil

Fry onions in oil until they are brown. Cut up the bacon and add it with the herbs and mushrooms and fry until the bacon is crisp. Meanwhile boil the rice in 3pt of salted water. Add the vinegar, sugar, mustard and stock to the gork with the chopped tomatoes. Let it simmer for 10 minutes. Before the rice is completely cooked, drain it and wash it in boiling water then stir it into the gork. Put it all into a casserole and sprinkle the cheese and nutmeg on top. Bake for 30 minutes in an oven at 180°C (350°F) Mark 4.

Couscous

The cheapest thing to eat in Paris, ubiquitous in the sleazy bistros of the Algerian quarter. You ate nothing else for six months once.

½lb couscous
2pt chicken stock
3 tbsp butter
salt and pepper
2 chicken pieces
1 large onion, chopped
3 tbsp oil
2 carrots, chopped
2 courgettes, chopped
4 tomatoes, peeled and chopped
2oz green beans
2oz artichoke hearts
6 whole peppercorns
1 tsp basil
¼ tsp ground cloves
1 tsp ground cummin
¼ tsp ground cinnamon
1 tsp sage
1 tsp paprika

Fry the onions and carrots roughly in oil. Add the chicken pieces and fry until they are brown. Add the other vegetables, spices, herbs and 1pt stock and simmer with the pan covered for 1¼ hours, stirring occasionally, and salting to taste. Meanwhile drown the couscous in cold water, 2in over the top and stir. When the grain has absorbed the water tip it into 1pt boiling stock. Cook for 15 minutes, stir in the butter and serve it at once in a separate dish from the ragout.

Liver and Bacon

Inexpensive and delicious, especially on cold nights when tiny hands tend to freeze.

1½lb lambs' or calves' liver
1 large onion, chopped
6 rashers streaky bacon
1 saucer cornflour
½ glass red wine
1 tbsp Worcestershire sauce
salt and pepper
2 tbsp tomato ketchup
1 tsp sage
1 tbsp butter

Fry the onion in butter until brown. Cut up the liver and roll each piece well in flour. Fry with the onion until it changes colour. Pour in ½pt water, add ketchup, sage and Worcestershire sauce and simmer for 30 minutes, seasoning to taste. Pour in the wine. Grill the bacon and lay it on top of the casserole. Reheat, covered, in a hot oven.

Hamburger Esterhazy

The first 'Bohemians' were fifteenth-century gypsies, wandering through France. Parisians assumed they had come from Bohemia; maybe you could persuade the lady that these two recipes did too.

1 large onion, chopped
1½lb best minced beef
¼lb button mushrooms
8 capers, chopped
5oz soured cream
salt and coarse black pepper
2 tsp paprika
1tsp coriander, ground
¼pt red wine
1 tbsp butter
1 tbsp Worcestershire sauce

Fry the onion in the butter until it is soft. Add the meat, salt and pepper, paprika, coriander, capers and mushrooms. When the meat is completely brown add the wine and Worcestershire sauce. To serve in the evening, remove it from the heat and keep it covered outside the fridge. Reheat by simmering for 10-15 minutes, stirring in the soured cream 5 minutes before serving.

Kraut

1 small red cabbage, chopped
1 medium-sized onion, chopped
3 tbsp wine vinegar
1 tsp green peppercorns
½ tbsp butter
1 heaped tbsp brown sugar
1 tsp nutmeg
salt and pepper
½pt water
½ apple, grated

Fry the onion in butter without letting it brown. Add the water, cabbage and the other ingredients, cover the saucepan for 30 minutes. Then uncover and continue simmering until all the excess water has evaporated.

Ratatouille

2 medium-sized onions, chopped
1 tsp oregano
1 tsp sage
3 peeled tomatoes
1lb aubergines
1lb courgettes
1lb green or yellow peppers
1 clove garlic
1 tbsp sugar
1 cup olive oil
1 tbsp wine vinegar
salt and pepper

Chop the aubergines and soak them for 1 hour in salted water. Crush the garlic and fry it with the onions in the oil until they begin to brown. Chop the tomatoes and add them together with the vinegar, sugar and chopped peppers. Chop the courgettes and put them, with the aubergines, into a pan of boiling water for 1 minute, then add with the herbs and salt and pepper to the melange. Simmer until the consistency suits you—vegetables soft but unbroken—stirring frequently. You may have to add a little water if it gets too dry. Like most stews, ratatouille is twice as good if cooked the day before it is eaten.

Drunken Peaches

2 large peaches
1/2 bottle white wine
2 tbsp honey
3in cinnamon stick
3 cloves
1/4 tsp grated nutmeg

Plunge the peaches into boiling water for 30 seconds, then peel and halve them and remove the stones. Crack the stones and take out the white kernels. Simmer the wine in a small pan with the kernels and spices without letting it boil. Stir in the honey and continue to simmer for 5 minutes. Remove the cloves, cinnamon and peach kernels and pour the liquor over the peaches. Allow to cool and serve with thick yellow cream.

Lemon Sorbet

4oz caster sugar
1/2pt water
1 egg white
juice of 1 1/2 lemons

Dissolve the sugar in the boiling water and simmer for 5 minutes. Pour it into a plastic bowl when it is cold, stir in the lemon juice, and put it in the freezer or ice-making part of the fridge until it is frozen to a mush. Beat the egg white into a foam. Quickly take out the mushy ice and beat it with a fork until it is smooth. Beat in the egg white, put it back in the bowl and let it freeze again. This takes hours, so make it, if you can, the night before.

A White Lady in the Straits

There are only a very few girls, pale, shy, ravaged by their addiction to cheap romance novels, for whom this evening is intended, but for that delicate minority it could prove fascinating. Their vision of the Far East is at once thrillingly vivid and shrouded in mysterious terrors; their hero, the man who has met the Orient face-to-face and preserved his standards intact.

Several prerequisites are important for success on this most difficult of evenings, and foremost amongst them is a talent for tall stories to rival the Ancient Mariner. It will be up to you to conjure an atmosphere worthy of Conrad and Maugham, to bring to life the sluggish currents of the South China Seas, the months monsoon-trapped on your verandah on a rubber plantation in Malaya, watching the river and the shrieking jungle while your Dayak houseboy brought you a gin stengah as darkness fell. There was bridge and tennis at the club thirty miles downriver by prahu, and for culture a few scratched records and a copy of *The Times,* six weeks old, but even on your own you dressed for dinner since, as the white tuan, certain things were expected. Mention the intolerable loneliness of the East and hint at a liaison with a lovely native girl, undertaken unconsciously to lay the ghost of the hopeless love that drove you out East in the first place, ending at last in honourable heartbreak.

The other requirement, unless you have money to spend, is access to the prop-room of a repertory company or a sale-or-return agreement with a well-furbished pawn shop. Even then a rattan peacock chair and an enormous ceiling fan may prove unobtainable, but try to borrow some silver dishes and napkin-rings to gleam on the stiff white tablecloth, a ceremonial kriss for the wall and a cigarette box fashioned from the skull of a tiger. They may serve to stimulate a yarn.

The ideal weather conditions for this soirée are to be found in England during August: then the muggy heat and torrential rain most closely approximate life in Burma or Kuala Solor (K.S. to you). Tidy your rooms completely, placing in positions of prominence anything white, bamboo or vaguely oriental, and, if you feel confident, erect a mosquito net about your bed. Fill the place with large tropical plants and turn the heaters on full, with bowls of water concealed beside them to promote a hothouse atmosphere. In front of your guest's cutlery floats an orchid in a silver dish.

Readers of Harlequin romances have, by definition, an extraordinarily high tolerance of the absurd; even so, great care must be taken about what to wear. A 'bum-freezer' mess-jacket can prompt derision from the most dedicated modern Lydia Languish, but baggy white trousers (for those with thin legs) or black dress trousers (for those without) cannot fail to please. Shoes should be conventional, black and highly polished, a cream-coloured silk shirt cufflinked and worn with a faded club tie. A white sharkskin jacket will add formality to the occasion without being stuffy.

It can be seen that this is an antique idiom, and we are assuming that the lady herself pays allegiance to convention where a suitor is concerned, on the surface at least. Use old-fashioned etiquette but beneath the rigid veneer hint at the dark, almost self-destructive impulses of your soul and offer it for salvation at the same time as you seek to bear her away, ecstatically irresponsible, on the tide of passion. Your behaviour may be flawless, but something of the unnameable mysteries of the jungle has remained within you and the hypnotic drums of Borneo beat in your heart. Within the context of gentility a loosening of the tie can appear frighteningly sensual.

So all is ready: the culinary temptations are keeping warm in the oven, the table gleams silver and white in the light of a pair of candles, and the other illuminations around the room are subtle. You have practised walking like a soldier and learned some exotic names from an atlas. The lady arrives. Greet her at the door with a bow so discreet as to be barely noticeable and as soon as maybe insinuate a cocktail into her hand. Mingle modest pleasantries with the merest hint of passionate impatience and lead her in the fullness of time to the dinner table by offering your arm. Such early physical contact makes things easier later on. Draw her out with questions and be fascinated by her replies, apologising that you are unaccustomed to a lady's company where you usually live and thus, with a becoming diffidence, embark upon your traveller's tales.

For background music start with late-nineteenth-century chamber music, progressing to Schubert and then, with the coffee, Mahler. Old 78rpm recordings such as you had up-river are preferable with their automatic sound effect of distant rain. When the time is ripe abandon words and, handing her to her feet, kiss her. Over the rest modesty must draw a careful veil.

There are certain problems with this idiom. The way of life it describes, apart from its inherent chauvinism, disappeared before the war and, on a more logical level, it is unlikely that a rubber-planter could cope with a dinner party without at least one houseboy. Should the lady raise these points you have two alternatives: bamboozle further and risk any hard-won credibility, or, smiling simply and with a sweet but brazen tact, change the subject.

MENU

Straits Sling

Nam Prik Pak
Chinese Patties
Stuffed Crab

Madurese Chicken Broth

Chicken Saté
Pork Sambal
Black-eyed Bean Curry
Broccoli Gulé

Brewer's Fruit

Coffee
Green Tea

Avoid consecutive chicken (a good rule of thumb on any occasion). The broth can be served with the main courses. Be prepared to sacrifice the pudding if you begin to feel bloated.

Straits Sling

8oz gin
2oz Benedictine
2oz cherry brandy
juice of 2 lemons
1 tsp angostura bitters
1 tsp orange bitters

Shake it all up with ice and serve it in long glasses, half and half with soda water.

Nam Prik Pak

This famous Thai creation makes a fascinating hors d'oeuvres. I have tried many variations on the sauce and find the following perversion of the traditional most acceptable. It's arranged like a course of crudités with a bowl of the sauce in the middle of a festival of raw vegetables cut into crisp, flat fingers. Any vegetable will do but aim for a variety of colours, textures and taste; for example, strips of unpeeled cucumber, courgettes, red, yellow and green sweet pepper, radish, carrot, celery, chicory, fennel root, cauliflower florets, bamboo shoots, sour apples, green beans, and any fresh edible flowers like nasturtium or white chrysanthemum petals. Deep-fry thin strips of banana in very hot oil until they are dark brown and scatter over the vegetables. The sauce:

1 tbsp butter
1 tbsp sambal trassie paste
2 tbsp Sajoer Lodeh paste
5oz plain yoghurt
juice of 1 lime

Chop the paste and fry in the butter with the sambal trassie. Simmer for 5 minutes then set aside to cool. After 15 minutes stir in the yoghurt and squeeze a lime over the top. Do not refrigerate. The pastes can be obtained from your local Indonesian grocer. As far as I know, the only one in England happens to be in Tooting High Street.

Chinese Patties

8oz plain sifted flour mixed with
½pt boiling water

Knead until it is no longer sticky and leave for 15 minutes.

1 large leek
½ tbsp butter
½lb chicken livers
1 tsp salt
½ tsp crushed ginger
½ tsp garlic powder
1 tsp black pepper
2 tbsp soya sauce

Chop leek very fine and brown in the butter. Chop livers very small and add. Mix in the spices. After 2 minutes mix in the soya sauce and cook until the livers are browned. On a floured board roll out the dough and cut out rounds 3in in diameter. Place 1 heaped tsp of livers on each and pinch up the dough into crescents. Deep fry in oil until they are golden brown. Serve with a small bowl of mango chutney and a sauce made by mixing . . .

3 tbsp tomato ketchup
2 tbsp mayonnaise
½ tsp nutmeg
1 tsp (or more to taste) ground chillies

Serve only four or five patties each: they are too tempting in abundance.

Stuffed Crab

1 large crab
1 leek
1 tbsp butter
½ tsp ground caraway seed
1 tsp ground ginger
salt and pepper

Have the fishmonger crack the crab and remove the external inedible parts. Once home, set to and extract the meat. Scoop out the brown flesh from the top of the shell, discarding the translucent membranes. Crack the core of the creature and scrape out the white meat, taking care not to include any of the fine white shell. Crack the claws and take out that meat too. Check it all for shell and set aside. Chop the leek very finely, wash it and fry it in the butter with the spices, without letting it brown. Mix it in with the crab meat. Season to taste, then pack the mixture back into the top of the shell. To eat, spoon it out onto thin brown toast.

Madurese Chicken Broth

Served between a starter and the main banquet, or as part of the banquet.

2 large chicken pieces
a few peeled prawns
1 tsp powdered ginger
½ tsp turmeric
1 medium-sized onion, chopped
salt and pepper
1 small clove garlic, crushed
juice of ½ lemon

Separate the meat from the bones. In a blender liquidise the onion, garlic, prawns, ginger, turmeric and lemon juice with as much water as you need to turn the blades. In a large saucepan cover the chicken bones with water and boil for 15 minutes, meanwhile soaking the meat in the blended melange. Add the meat and melange to the soup with a little more water to cover it and simmer for 1½ hours. Remove the bones and season with salt and pepper. Remove the meat, slice it finely and return to the broth. Serve with a small bowl of rice and a wee dish of hot pickle.

Chicken Saté

- 3 skinned chicken breasts
- 3 tbsp soya sauce
- ½ tsp salt
- 2 tbsp water
- ½ tsp ground caraway seed
- ½ tsp ground clove
- ½ tsp ground nutmeg
- 1 tsp black pepper

Cut the chicken into 1in cubes, rub in the spices and soak them in the liquids for 3 hours. Thread 5 pieces onto each of a dozen or so wooden skewers and grill or, more conveniently, put the skewers in a dish with the remains of the liquid and bake for 1 hour at 200°C (400°F) Mark 6. Make the sauce and cook it separately. It really does taste better the next day, heated in the oven with the chicken.
The sauce:

- 1 large onion, chopped
- ⅓ tsp ground chillies
- 4 tbsp shredded coconut
- 1in piece of lemon peel
- 1 tbsp lemon juice
- 2 tbsp sunflower oil
- 4oz crunchy peanut butter
- 4 tbsp soya sauce
- 4 tbsp water
- 1 clove garlic, crushed

Fry onion in oil until brown. Put it with the oil and all the other ingredients, except the peanut butter and the soya sauce, into a blender and blend until smooth. Put in a pan and stir in the peanut butter and soya sauce and simmer for 10 minutes. Bake in the oven as mentioned above. Serve the sauce in a bowl with a small dish of pickled vegetables.

Pork Sambal

My variation of a straits Chinese dish.

- 1oz chicken fat or butter
- 2 large pork chops
- 2 large leeks
- 1 heaped tsp ground ginger
- 1 tsp ground chillies
- 1 tsp ground caraway seed
- 1 heaped tsp salt
- ½ tsp dried mint
- 1 2in cinnamon stick
- ¼pt water
- juice of ½ lemon

Remove all fat and bones from the pork chops and cut the meat into thin slices. Chop leeks very finely and fry them in the fat in a casserole, stirring in the ginger, chillie powder, caraway seed, salt and mint. When it begins to stick, stir in the water, meat and the cinnamon stick. Simmer uncovered for 30 minutes. Just before serving, remove the cinnamon and stir in the lemon juice.

Black-eyed Bean Curry

1lb tin of black-eyed beans
1 medium-sized onion, chopped
3 tbsp oil or butter
2 tsp sugar
4oz yoghurt
1 tsp ground coriander
½ tsp ground allspice
½ tsp powdered lemongrass
½ tsp powdered garlic
salt

Brown the onion in the oil. Mix in the spices and stir, frying for 3 minutes. Tip in the beans in their liquor and cook in the oven for 1 hour at 200°C (400°F) Mark 6. Add a little water if it gets too dry. Stir in the yoghurt (or soured cream) 5 minutes before serving.

Broccoli Gulé

9oz broccoli
5 spring onions
1in piece ginger
1 tbsp crushed almonds
½ tsp turmeric
½ tsp powdered lemongrass
1 tsp sambal trassie paste
10oz tin thick coconut milk

Put everything except the broccoli in a frying pan and bring to the boil, stirring all the time. After about 10 minutes when it begins to reduce add the broccoli and simmer for a further 10 minutes. Reheat it, covered, in the oven.

Brewer's Fruit

4 large bananas
1 miniature black rum
5 tbsp brown sugar
juice of 1 lime

Peel bananas. Lay them in an ovenproof dish. Pour on the rum and lime juice, sprinkle on the sugar. Cover the dish with tinfoil and bake for 45 minutes in an oven at 200°C (400°F) Mark 6. Try to remember to remove the tinfoil for the last 15 minutes. Serve with thick yellow cream, and a peeled orange, divided into segments.

Pilau Talk

'Would you like to come around tonight and maybe listen to some music?' The girl to whom this apparently innocent question is addressed is an intellectual, caught at the moment of self-doubt when literary criticism is seeming cold and unreal; the would-be host is a being from another world, compassionate, sincere, a man whose karma is calmer. To the like-minded group with whom he exclusively associates he is something of a guru, partly because he can relate to their ids, mostly because he has actually *been* to India.

This will be a short-lived affair. Initially fascinating, the mellow hippy grows stale very quickly to people outside his aura. His complete detatchment from the intellect becomes wearing and his naive view of life infuriates. For one night, though, life in the bubble of peace can seem remarkably enticing.

If you live alone, try and give the impression that you don't. Imply that your flat is a commune by leaving several pairs of wet jeans drying in the bath. Hide all technology except the record-player, and move chairs and sofas out of the room after taking off their cushions to use as seats, for everything must be at floor height. Table lamps and candles are set on the carpet and bricks are book-ends along the skirting, sandwiching popular classics like *Siddhartha, Zen and the Art, Catch 22* and picture books of Bosch. Records are scattered everywhere; the room is clean but incredibly untidy.

During the afternoon before she arrives, burn joss-sticks in the kitchen so that their aroma is a mere hint in the air. Invest in a second-hand Buddha. Bath, don't shave, and if your hair is long enough, part it in the middle and fasten it in a pony-tail with a rubber-band, but try not to touch it during the evening. If, on the other hand, you have short hair resist the temptation to buy a wig and avoid false beards; they can only lead to paranoia or worse, if, temporarily forgotten, a mat of artificial locks should slip from your head into the curry.

It is conceivable that you took orange while in India. Many return as acolytes of Light in saffron robes; the streets of Earls Court are abustle with disciples who have compromised between faith and climate and now wear russet jeans, ochre parkas and tangerine wool hats. Otherwise, try a white collarless shirt outside baggy jeans or white cotton

trousers and nothing on your feet. Get into the frame of mind by talking to yourself, addressing yourself throughout as 'man'.

You are sensitive, open and naive, and possessed of a genuine humanitarian compassion sadly diluted by a tendency to relax for months on end. In India you were searching for yourself through religion, though you have no actual knowledge of it, just an appreciation of the essence. You help people out selflessly, take children to the zoo, and meditate of an afternoon, not transcendentally, just sitting in a room with the record-player going and thinking.

A sophisticated impersonation should include a seed or two of self-doubt: a hardly realised fear that people find you ultimately shallow. For this reason you create the atmosphere of a test as you entertain the lady, suggesting silently that she take you as you are. By going on about your group, its integration and integrity, make her feel that if she ends up not belonging it is because she is hung-up and cold. Try and produce in her a feeling of challenge by referring to all the girls you know platonically; if she is attracted to you, she will seek about for ways to mean more than they. Toast her once as you sit down to eat by saying 'To Radha'. If she is puzzled or asks about drama schools, explain that Radha was the girl whom Krishna loved in his youth. After that make no more reference to sex until the end of the evening. Then, just as she has finished talking about one of her enthusiasms, open your eyes wide and in your sincerest voice remark: 'I'd really like to make love with you', conjuring into the words all your philosophy of natural companionship, your relaxed attitude to bodies.

There are certain things that you relate to in a special way; the music of Neil Young, The Band and Shaun Phillips, the pictures of Escher which you saw in a shop and immediately 'reached', and the Cantonese wind-flute which you make noises on but cannot play. You refer to eating as 'breaking bread together' and have substituted the sharing of experience for wit.

Too lazy to ever take that summer job you mention, you went overland to India with a few things in a carpetbag and met a lot of really amazing people. One day you will go back to the temple but not until a lot of the stuff in your mind is sorted out, meanwhile there are your memories, hazy recollections of smells for the most part with a few esoteric place names thrown in for good measure. Also, you learnt how to cook and to eat with your fingers. This could take practice so rehearse using a paratha (see p.37) in your left hand and the first three fingers of your right as a spoon, soaking up wet curries with rice. Have a finger bowl in the middle of the other dishes and use it once early on in the meal to avoid confusion.

In presenting the banquet a little atypical psychology might not come amiss. Serve the mooroongakai first on their own, putting the plates down on a cloth spread out on the floor. All alone, they will engender sudden doubt in the mind of your guest, memories of tales of nauseating macrobiotic starvation amongst the fashionable. Once eaten, bring in all the other things together and when she smiles again explain the trick and boost your rating in the honesty stakes. Serve red wine from start to finish and orange pekoe tea.

One last recreation might be effective but it requires all the laid-back confidence this man can muster. Indian grandmothers do it to their newly born descendants: before the meal, dip your finger in honey and write the word OM on the lady's tongue. Mystic.

MENU

Mooroongakai

Chicken Biriani or Chicken Koormah
Prawn and Pilchard Curry or Fish Moilee
Lady's Fingers
Dahl
Parathas
Raw Chutney
Cucumber Raita

Kulfi

Tea

Few decisions to be made here, but if you decide to serve Chicken Koormah the meal will also need rice. Find a light red wine like a young Beaujolais. With the tea bring out a little bowl of spicy breath-sweeteners called supari.

Mooroongakai (Drumsticks)

These subtle and delicious vegetables are worth the trouble of finding. Indian greengrocers are the people to approach. Chop off the ends and cut the drumsticks into 3in lengths. Boil them in salted water for 10 minutes and serve them as they are, splitting each and scraping the inner flesh off against your teeth as if they were artichoke leaves. Have a finger bowl of rose-scented water nearby.

Chicken Biriani

Fantastic looking, birianis are not as difficult to create as people would have you believe. It's really done by combining simple things into an elaborate mosaic of flavours. Follow the recipe for chicken koormah but cut the meat up into small pieces—½ tsp of crushed garlic can be added to the marinade if you like. After it has done its initial hour in the oven, set it aside. Meanwhile . . .

a pt glass, ¾ full of dry patna rice
½ tsp turmeric
2oz chopped onion
½oz broken cashew nuts
2 tbsp sultanas
1 tbsp butter
½ tsp ground cloves
½ tsp ground cinnamon
½ tsp ground caraway seed
2 bay leaves
1 tsp ground cummin
salt

Boil the rice and the turmeric in 3pt of salted water, with the bay leaves. While that is cooking, fry the onion in the butter until it begins to burn, then add the sultanas and the rest of the spices with 3 tsp salt. Fry them until they have soaked up the butter and a heady smell pervades the kitchen. Set them aside. When the rice is cooked, drain it and wash it in 3 kettlesful of boiling water. Drain it again, then mix it with the chicken koormah and the spicy onions. Heat it up uncovered in a hot oven and serve it on a very big shallow dish, garnished with the cashew nuts and a sprinkling of poppy seeds.

Chicken Koormah

Subtlest of 'curries', this will not startle the throat or prompt indigestion, a malady which is only equalled by the common cold as a foe to love.

1 tbsp butter
1 medium-sized onion, chopped
3 chicken breasts, skinned and boned
8oz soured cream
juice of 1 lemon
1oz pine nuts
1 tsp poppy seed
1 tbsp ground coriander
4 tsp salt
1 tsp ground caraway seed
1 tsp ground chillies
1 tsp powdered ginger
½ tsp ground nutmeg
½ tsp ground allspice

Melt the butter in a heavy casserole and cook the onion until it begins to brown. Remove from the heat and put in 6oz of soured cream and all the other ingredients, covering the chicken. Leave it for 2 hours to marinade, then put on the lid and cook it in the oven for 1 hour at 200°C (400°F) Mark 6. Do this in the morning or, better still, the day before. Reheat in the oven for 30 minutes without a lid, stirring a couple of times. Just before you serve it, stir in the rest of the soured cream.

Prawn and Pilchard Curry

Like many of the brethren of the communes this curry appears exotic but its heart is usually canned.

½lb prawns, shelled
1lb tin pilchards in tomato sauce
1 large onion, chopped
1 tbsp vinegar
1 tsp sugar
1 tbsp butter
1 tbsp ground coriander
½ tbsp turmeric
½ tbsp ground cummin
2 tsp salt
½-1 tsp ground chillies
1 tsp ground ginger
2 tsp ground allspice
2 tomatoes, chopped
3 tbsp oil or ghee

Fry the onion in the butter in a heavy casserole until soft. Mix in the spices, stirring constantly, and dribbling in 2 tbsp water. Stir in the sugar and vinegar and simmer for 5 minutes, adding enough water to prevent it sticking. Carefully stir in the prawns and pilchards with all their sauce. Drop 3 tbsp oil or ghee onto the top and cook, uncovered, in an oven for 1¼ hours at 200°C (400°F) Mark 6. Fifteen minutes before serving add the chopped tomatoes.

Fish Moilee

A Goanese recipe of great delicacy. Any large-flaked fish can be used but smoked haddock works particularly well.

3 smoked haddock fillets
1 medium-sized onion, chopped
1 tbsp butter
½ coconut, grated
6oz tin thick coconut milk
2 tomatoes, chopped
⅓pt milk
1½in piece fresh ginger
4 fresh green chillies
1 tbsp wine vinegar
1 tsp turmeric
½ tsp ground caraway seed
½ tsp ground cinnamon
1 tsp garam masala

Separate the skinned fish into small pieces. Mix vinegar with all the spices except the garam masala. Slice the ginger and the chillies. Fry onion in the butter until soft, then add ginger, chillies and spice mixture. Stir and simmer over a very low flame for 3 minutes. Stir in the milk, coconut and coconut milk, reserving some of the grated coconut as a garnish. Bring to the boil, stirring, then put in the fish and tomatoes. Do not stir. Set aside. When ready to serve, reheat it, covered, for 30 minutes in an oven at 200°C (400°F) Mark 6, again without stirring. Sprinkle on the coconut and the garam masala just before you eat it.

Lady's Fingers

Much more delicious than stewing them, and less complicated. Ask at an Indian or West Indian grocers for behndi or okra.

½lb lady's fingers
1 tbsp butter
3 spring onions
½ tsp ground chillies
salt

Immerse the lady's fingers in boiling water for 3 minutes then scrape each one clean of excess stickiness and stringiness. Fry them in the butter with the finely chopped spring onions, sprinkling on the chillies and salt to taste, until they begin to brown.

Dahl

Especially with a biriani and therefore no rice, dahl forms a sound basis for a meal as well as a subtle vegetable. The temptation is to make and eat too much of them, leaving no room for the other curries. Experiment with your own combinations of spices, the following is just one variation.

¼lb dry dahl lentils
½ tbsp butter
½ medium-sized onion, chopped
1 tsp ground coriander
1 tsp turmeric
tiny pinch ground chillies

1 tbsp white vinegar	½ clove garlic, crushed
salt	4 whole cloves

Soak the lentils in salted water overnight. Rinse thoroughly and boil them in ¾pt water. Brown the onion and garlic in the butter, then add the vinegar and spices, stirring constantly. When they begin to stick pour in the dahl and liquid. Bring to the boil. Cool in an oven, uncovered, for 45 minutes at 200°C (400°F) Mark 6, adding a tbsp or two of milk if it looks too dry. Garnish with slices of tomato, fresh mint or parsley.

Parathas

Since these serve as a spoon when eating with your fingers, make five or six. Tear a piece off and hold it in your left hand, using it to push together a little rice and some curry. (You should heap your plate with all the different foods at the same time.) Scoop up the mouthful with the first three fingers of your right hand. When the paratha piece becomes sodden with gravy, eat that and tear off another piece.

8oz fine wholewheat flour	4 tbsp melted butter
2 tsp salt	oil and water

Mix salt and flour and knead in three-quarters of the butter, adding a little water until it is a pliable dough. Pull off little pieces and roll them into golf balls, then, with a rolling pin or claret bottle, flatten each one paper thin. Put a tsp of butter on each and spread it, then pile the sheets four-high. Roll out again as thin as possible and trim the edges to form a disc. Sprinkle with hardly any salt. Barely moisten the bottom of a clean frying pan with oil and fry each paratha slowly, without allowing them quite to blacken.

Raw Chutney

This is surprisingly cooling with the curries, but because of the raw onion, make sure she eats some too.

2 firm tomatoes, chopped small	1 tbsp sugar
1 large onion, chopped small	½ tsp powdered cloves
¼pt wine vinegar	½ tsp powdered ginger
salt and red pepper	1 tsp green peppercorns

Mix everything together in a bowl 2 hours before you are going to eat it. Until then, cover the bowl with clinging plastic.

Mango Chutney

Always buy Mango chutney.

Cucumber Raita

1 small cucumber
5oz yoghurt
2 leaves mint, chopped
pinch ground cummin
salt and pepper
1/4 tsp paprika

Peel and chop the cucumber finely. Stir well into the yoghurt with the very finely chopped mint, cummin and salt and pepper. Sprinkle the paprika (or cayenne) on top.

Kulfi

Making kulfi is a long process and there are no real short-cuts to take. This is a recipe for a sort of ice cream that bears some resemblance to the real thing. A perfect and digestive end to the meal.

1 block vanilla ice cream
10 cardamon pods
2 tbsp slivered pistachio nuts or almonds
1/4 drop rose essence
1/4 tsp powdered cinnamon

Use the whitest 'Italian-style' ice cream. Put it in a bowl and wait for it to soften. Split each pod and extract the seeds. Crush them to a powder and beat them with the nuts and cinnamon into the soft ice cream. Use only the merest hint of rose essence by dropping it onto the fork and shaking it off then stirring the ice cream some more. Spoon the mixture into individual soufflé dishes or conical moulds and put them in the ice-making part of the fridge for at least 3 hours.

A Stiff Manhattan

To the Doris Days and Gloria Grahames of this world this most unattractive manifestation of the solo male has always proved irresistible. He is an international phenomenon, born in the fifties, secretly controlling the sixties, absolute ruler of the seventies, but seems at his most powerful today and nowhere more than in New York. He is the urban superbachelor, a connoisseur, the liberal Democrat who votes Republican, the avowed feminist who treats women as executive toys.

From the immaculate wall-to-wall ego of his penthouse apartment he gazes down at Manhattan's streets, eagle-eyed and predatory, obsessed with the impression he makes. He is in advertising or some other promotional game that forces him to work incredibly hard for enormous sums of money. Perhaps he had a wife who suffered a nervous breakdown when he divorced her and now lives in San Francisco; he fancies himself charming and cruel, self-sufficient and always in command.

Very few normal homes lend themselves to conversion into a pad of this man's calibre, but the effect can be approached by taking everything but the carpets out of a room. Move back the sofa, tables and hard back chairs, shelve the books as decor rather than reading material, install the hi-fi neatly with the speakers concealed. As the focal point of the room add a cocktail cabinet; this man is an expert at food and drink and to see him mixing a Black Russian is to sense his power. It keeps him walking round the room as well, showing off his jogger's fitness, his designer trousers, and allowing him to dominate a seated guest. Hide all other furniture in another room.

In this role you collect modern art: a few undiscovered investment painters whom you patronise and some more established American cubists. As an example of your wry humour you have a Chagall in the hall.

It is easy to fake trendy paintings: take a piece of white paper, 3 × 4 feet, and lay it flat on a table. Drop one tablespoon of brown ink into the middle and move it carefully about to form a shape about ten inches in diameter. Then sop up the wet ink from the middle of the shape with kitchen towel. Frame and hang having first written 'Schauss 3/20' near the bottom in pencil. Towards the same end buy any piece of car engine from a scrapyard, polish it and mount it on a block of wood and place it with reverence in a promi-

nent place. If the lady refers to it, and there will be few other conversation pieces in your austere flat, feign surprise that she doesn't recognise it; there is, after all, a copy in the Guggenheim.

A fascist where sex is concerned, you have taken advantage of the feminist movement to shrug off much of the etiquette of seduction. As soon as your guest has arrived and is seated, move to the slim hi-fi near the books and take off the Telemann flute music you have been playing for your own amusement, putting on instead a record of Ella Fitzgerald or Irving Berlin. Mix a Martini ostentatiously by pouring vodka (prepared a week before by putting the peel of a lemon into the bottle and leaving it in the fridge) into a tumbler of ice and adding two drops of vermouth. Transfer the elixir without the ice into cocktail glasses. Before you sit down, close the portfolio of work that lies open on your desk. Now engage in this cad's mating ritual: stare at her intently with a half-smile playing about your lips. Make no initial attempt at conversation but answer her with smooth self-confidence referring every subject to yourself. Your hobbies are squash, photography (all your photographs and equipment are in New York) and of course you have a pilot's licence. Your friends are all men, working in the media or Washington, your interest in the Arts limited to the new movement towards American expression in the work of some off-Broadway theatre companies and a few artists like the mythical Schauss, though you are familiar with absolutely everything. Your attitude to Europe is patronising: its heritage is still valid, but it has ceased to be innovative.

Confidence is everything in this guise; a moment's fumble and the whole glittering monstrous ego is shattered, but with sufficient self-satisfaction anything can be achieved. All other approaches having met with smug assurance the lady might just be desperate enough to turn to sex as the last remaining opportunity to dominate, excite or destroy you.

Clothes are a problem tonight. Everything has to be casual but obviously expensive: soft leather shoes, beautifully but conventionally cut soft corduroy trousers, a new shirt and a jacket of cashmere or camel-coloured velvet, conservative but relaxed.

In a foreign country you are an ambassador of American culture, and the food you have cooked tonight is part of that, New England seafood, the mythical dishes of diners on route sixteen, the trendy junk of the very chic Manhattan parties. Fast-food some of it may be, but you serve it in beautiful dishes and bowls and accompany the meal with outrageously expensive French wine (plonk in a decanter or an empty bottle begged from a restaurant), followed by perfect brandy and coffee, to the strains of Art Tatum or Johnny Hodges: cool jazz at the best of times but coupled with your chilling smile should she dare to argue and your habit of staring at her body when she's trying to make a conversational point, positively arctic. Whatever your true devotion, in this guise you see a woman as a whore, through some atavistic memory of the Puritan fathers, and your eyes give you away. After such behaviour it will be no good suddenly peeling off the mask, giggling and explaining the evening's game; you might well find yourself with a Schauss

sticking out of your head and not a court in the land but would call it justifiable homicide. So resist any temptation to be nice. Just narrow your eyes and grin.

MENU

Clam Chowder or Vichysoisse

Kipper Paté or Chili

Meatloaf
Pocketbook Steak
Rack of Lamb
Caesar Salad

Fake Crème Brûlée
Hot Cheesecake

Coffee, Brandy

Chili is also a possible entrée; sweet potatoes are suggested as a vegetable (p. 57). If you decide on Clam Chowder avoid a consecutive fish dish, and a juxtaposition of chili with meatloaf or steak might be too much of a good thing.

Clam Chowder

Be a New England clam bore: extol the virtues of razor clams above cherrystones, littlenecks or quahogs.

1 9oz tin clams
3 rashers smoked bacon
1 small onion, chopped fine
1 large potato, sliced thin
½pt single cream
½pt salt water
2 tbsp butter
salt and black pepper
1 tsp chopped parsley
¼ tsp cayenne pepper

Drain the clam liquor into a cup. Grill bacon until crisp. Melt one tbsp butter in a pan and brown the onion. Boil salted water and cook the potatoes until they are soft. Crumble the bacon into the potato and its water and add the onion, clam liquor, salt and pepper to taste, and simmer for 5 minutes. Pour in the cream, return to the boil and set it aside. When you want to serve it, bring it back to the boil, tip in the clams and simmer for 2 minutes. Pour it into an elegant tureen and sprinkle on the cayenne and parsley. Serve with crackers.

Have vichysoisse in the fridge and ask subtly whether she is allergic to shellfish. If she is, give her vichysoisse but have chowder yourself.

Vichysoisse

It can only help to stimulate your confidence to know that you are starting the meal with a perfect soup.

2 tbsp butter
2 leeks
½ large onion, chopped
1 fist-sized potato
1½ chicken stock cubes
½ pinch nutmeg
5 drops Worcestershire sauce
3oz double cream
salt and pepper
1½pt hot water

Chop up the white part of the leeks and fry them in the butter with the onion until they are soft. Cut the potato into very small slices. Dissolve the stock cubes in the water and add to the onion with nutmeg and Worcestershire sauce, put in the potato and cook it slowly until the potato is soft. Cool it a little then blend briefly until it is smooth. Add salt and pepper to taste. Refrigerate until you're ready to eat then stir in the cream thoroughly. Serve it in tiny delicate bowls.

Kipper Paté

2lb kipper fillets
6 tbsp butter
½ cup double cream
juice of 1 lemon
pinch of salt
1 tsp garlic powder
3 tsp mild paprika
2 tsp black pepper
1 tbsp Worcestershire sauce
2 tbsp oregano

Boil the kippers for 10 minutes. Carefully peel off the skin and any excess bones. The thin 'hair' bones can be left. Melt the butter slowly with 1 tbsp water in a heavy pan. In a basin mix 4 tbsp of the butter, 2 tsp of the paprika and all the other ingredients, very thoroughly. Press down firmly. Over the flat surface pour the rest of the butter and sprinkle the top with 1 tsp of paprika. Refrigerate. Remove from the fridge at least 1 hour before serving. Offer brown toast with it.

Chili

In little bowls this is a chic first course, in bigger ones it offers an opportunity for lies about the little town in Mexico where you got your first divorce.

1 large onion, chopped
2 tbsp oil
1lb best minced beef
3oz tomato puree
½pt beef stock
1 15oz tin kidney beans
2 tbsp white vinegar
1 flat tbsp powdered chillies
¼pt water
salt

Fry the onion in the oil until it is soft. Add the mince and fry until it is brown. Spoon off as much of the fat as you can. Add the rest of the ingredients (using the water if it becomes too dry) and simmer for 30 minutes. Taste it and think about adding more chilli, remembering that its flavour will develop if you leave it for a while before reheating. Serve it with a pile of water biscuits.

Meatloaf

Delicious hot, or cold on hot nights, this is a dish with a subtle machismo.

1lb minced beef
½lb minced veal
½lb pork sausage meat
1 large leek, chopped fine
2 eggs, beaten
6 stuffed olives
3 tsp salt
1 tsp black pepper
½ tsp ground mace
1 tsp thyme
1½ slices brown bread
3 tbsp milk
2 tsp Worcestershire sauce
4 rashers lean bacon

Soak the crumbled bread in the milk and mix it, in a basin, with all the other ingredients, except the bacon. Line a pyrex casserole with the bacon and press the mixture tightly in. Place it on a baking tray to catch any fugitive fat and bake it for 1 hour and 20 minutes in an oven at 180°C (350°F) Mark 4. Take it out, holding a wooden spoon across the top to prevent the meatloaf falling out and drain off the excess fat (keep it for the sauce). Then tip it out onto a plate, garnish with parsley and serve. Otherwise, let it cool and carve it cold, in which case it is sometimes called Cut-and-come-again. Serve it with either of the following sauces, both of which, incidentally, are good with steak.

2oz chopped onion
fat from the meatloaf
¾lb tin tomatoes
salt and pepper
3 tsp cornflour
1 tsp oregano

Fry the onion in the fat until it is soft then stir in the flour thoroughly. Stir in the other ingredients and simmer for 15 minutes. Or, more interestingly . . .

fat from the meatloaf
3 tbsp Dijon mustard
1 tsp green peppercorns
2oz double cream
salt and pepper

In a small pan reheat the fat and stir in the mustard, peppercorns, salt and pepper. After a few minutes simmering add the cream and simmer for 1 minute more.

Pocketbook Steak

2 large, thick, entrecôte steaks
2 dozen oysters
3 tbsp cream
salt and black pepper
2 tbsp butter
2oz fine golden breadcrumbs
1 tbsp Worcestershire sauce
1 tsp tarragon

Steaks have to be cooked on the spot. There is really no way of getting round this fact, but the Manhattan is insolent enough to spend a little time in the kitchen. Prepare what you can in advance, however. Roll the oysters in breadcrumbs and fry in 1 tbsp butter for 3 minutes, tossing continually. Set aside, ready to use. Mix the tarragon, cream and Worcestershire sauce in a cup. Beg the butcher to slit a pocket in the steaks when you buy them, or do it yourself with a very sharp knife, slitting along the side to make a pouch. Flatten the steaks a little and rub them with salt and pepper. When the time comes, melt the butter in a very hot frying pan and fry the steaks until dark brown on each side. Put the oysters into the pan and fry for 2 more minutes with the steak. Working in the pan, stuff each steak with as many oysters as possible, and serve up on hot plates. With the heat on full, stir in the cream mixture with the meat juices, bring to the boil and pour over the steaks.

Rack of Lamb

Roasting meat is the easiest way of cooking it, but the results will depend more on the quality of the meat to begin with than upon your skill, so spend a few extra pennies on going to a really good butcher. This cut is great with the leek and potato recipe found in the vegetables section (p. 57) and a simple gravy.

1lb best end of neck of lamb (with or without chine bone)
1 tsp rosemary
salt

Rub the meat with rosemary and salt and place on a grill over a baking tin in an oven for 40 minutes at 200°C (400°F) Mark 6. Put some small tomatoes or mushrooms in the tin if you like. Gravy:

3 tbsp fat from lamb or other meat
1 flat tbsp cornflour
2 tsp salt
2/3pt water
2 tbsp Worcestershire sauce
1 tsp oregano

Stir flour into hot fat to a paste. Stir in water and other ingredients. Bring to the boil and allow to bubble for 3 minutes. Decant into gravy boat.

Caesar Salad

2 heads Bibb lettuce
1/2pt mug white bread cubes
12 tbsp olive oil
3 garlic cloves, chopped
12 anchovy fillets, chopped
1 tsp salt
juice of 1 lemon
1 tsp black pepper
1 egg
6oz grated parmesan

Heat 4 tbsp oil in a pan with the garlic. Drop in the bread croutons and fry until brown and crisp. Remove croutons but not garlic. Break the lettuce into bite-sized bits and wash well. Dry it, then toss it in your salad bowl with 8 tbsp oil. Add the croutons, salt, pepper, anchovies and lemon juice. Carry into the dining room with the egg and the cheese in a little bowl. Flamboyantly break the egg over the lettuce and toss it all a good deal, then sprinkle on the parmesan, smiling casually.

Fake Crème Brûlée

Long sought after by greedy incompetents keen to impress.

1 sachet vanilla cream dessert	4 tbsp water
1pt milk	4oz muscovado sugar
½pt double cream	fruit

In a small, beautiful, ovenproof dish scatter the fruit of your choice—halved grapes, stoned cherries, sliced bananas or apples, etcetera. Whip the cream until it is very stiff. Follow the directions for making the dessert. (Use the kind that calls for cold milk as others contain too much flour.) When it is nearly set, fold in the cream and pour it all over the fruit. Put it in the fridge for 1 hour. Sprinkle the top liberally with the sugar, covering completely, and put it under the grill, watching until the sugar melts. Put it back in the fridge.

Hot Cheesecake

Halfway between a cheesecake and a soufflé—it's how this cad describes his first wife.

1 tbsp melted butter	2 tbsp caster sugar
3 digestive biscuits	½ tsp vanilla essence
4oz cottage cheese	2 tsp cornflour
5oz cream cheese	3oz soured cream
2 eggs, separated	

In two individual soufflé dishes crumble the biscuits and pour on melted butter, patting the mixture down hard. In a bowl mix the cheeses, sugar, vanilla and egg yolks. Sprinkle on the cornflour and carry on mixing, adding the soured cream. Beat the egg whites into a froth and fold them in well. Pour the mixture into the dishes and bake for 1 hour at 150°C (300°F) Mark 2. Let them cool and stand for a few hours and they turn into cheesecake, but hot they are rather more unusual.

The Romance of the Roes

Moral blackmail has always featured in an inventory of Cupid's arsenal, and few seducers have used the weapon to such effect as the medieval troubadour. Surely the original purpose of all those extravagant claims of lovesickness and threats of suicide, the poker-faced assertions that some worldly chatelaine was as chaste and perfect as the Virgin, was to shame the lady into bed by pointing up the absurdity of denial. Ultimately, with only the verse surviving, without the twinkle in the singer's eye, what started as a game of subtle irony was seen as serious, turned into philosophy by dour Burgundians with muscular wives from Bath checking what they wrote each night. Ignore them. Tonight you must take your character from the jolly jongleur whose brethren died in the Albigensian wars. Talk as if you had been there.

The preparation for a medieval evening calls for some resourcefulness. First of all there is the important issue of the invitation: with black ink on a sheet of pale green paper compose or copy a sonnet, ending it with the sentiment that should the lady refuse to appear for dinner on a certain date the poet will terminate his life. Attach this, unsigned, to a white rose and leave it somewhere where she alone will find it. Next day, repeat the entreaty, fixing the letter to a slightly pinker flower and using a different sonnet; work in-

to the lyric instructions for how she can reply. This should continue every day, the flowers getting pinker, until finally your invitation is accepted. This could take time, so open an account at a florists and buy a copy of Petrarch, but the day will come when she will say yes, if only to find out whom her mysterious correspondent could be. From then until the appointed evening compose ecstatic odes to joy in violet ink on pure white paper and fix them to roses of the deepest red, remaining anonymous but including your address in the final poem.

To help in this difficult and tedious pursuit, you could begin to transform your bedroom, for it is here that you will entertain. Move your hi-fi speakers up to the ceiling and fill your shelves with old bound books. Buy a vast amount of crimson or dark-blue cloth and nail it all the way round the room at the height of the top of the door, then gather it together in the middle of the ceiling and fasten it so as to seem like the inside of a knightly pavilion. Hide all tables and chairs and drape any remaining modern furniture with old velvet curtains. Borrow thirty cushions and scatter them upon the bed and floor, and fill the room with bowls of potpourri, tiny mirrors, glassware and about twenty dim candles, the sort that lurk in craters of wax. The whole effect should be one of Saracen opulence, with every inch of wall and floor covered by tapestries or old rugs.

All this decadence will be offset by your burning, youthful energy, Bath and shave and dress like a crusader on a quiet night in, with a floor-length white kaftan, belted, and a pair of thong sandals. Join a record library and make up an endless tape of lute music, Monteverdi madrigals and even a little Gregorian chant.

So the room is ready, each of the four or five courses you have prepared is set out in the kitchen or waiting in the oven, wooden plates, knives and two-pronged forks are concealed ready in the bedroom and the wine is waiting in an exquisite crystal jug. On to the first problem: the door-bell rings, you answer it and watch the lady's face fall from curiosity to hostile annoyance. She may say something like 'You!' or 'Oh God!' Do not be dismayed. Before she can back away into the night, take her hand and kiss it, apologise for the anonymity of the invitations and lead her into the bedroom. A friend of mine relates how his beloved's image of him as a sporting hearty was immediately jeopardised when confronted with the decor. He explained how he had languished with love of her so long and been driven to exorcise his despair on the muddy fields of organised sport; she looked, she listened, she laughed, and accepted a glass of golden wine.

Helping the lady into this fantasy can be made easier with a few good stories. Have on the tip of your tongue poetic versions of the tales of Aucassin and Nicolette, Osberne and Elfhild, and incite her to ask about them by calling her by the ladies' names. Rehearse these narrations in a mirror and tell them well, with enthusiasm dressed in modest humour.

When the time comes to eat, seat her on a pile of cushions before a very low table of old dark wood. Serve several different types of wine from jugs or labelless bottles and only supply coffee if she insists on it. After the meal, move the table away to the side of the room without all the palaver of clearing plates away into the kitchen and press your suit upon her.

This is a time of some delicacy. Missing the moment when your guest is expectant of action is as clumsy as misjudging it, and a physical gap unbridged tends to widen. Kissing her hand again will lead nowhere but you could remind her that you are a clerk learned in spells and offer to read her palm, or better still, in honour of the maytime, produce a rose from somewhere and carefully fasten it in her hair.

The melancholy that was so moving in your early epistles is invariably boring in the flesh. Hint at the responsibility the lady bears for your very existence, but only once and at the beginning of the evening; otherwise channel your love into changes of mood, exuberantly passionate, charmingly shy, though never coy, and try to be in love with all things. Whatever happens, you will both have enjoyed yourselves and an evening in the Languedoc can sometimes work wonderful miracles. It did for my friend. To the delight of all, he never played rugby again.

MENU

Mouse Soup
Herb Bread

Golden Quarrels or Small Pies

Dragon's Tail
Roast Pheasant
Spicey Rabbit

Fish in Weeds
Roe Broth

Rosee
Gilded Gingerbread

Serve only tiny amounts of the first two courses and choose vegetables that were around before the sixteenth century: parsnips rather than potatoes, turnips before tomatoes.

Mouse Soup

Not really mice . . .

¾lb mushrooms
1 medium-sized onion, chopped
½pt chicken stock
½ tsp sugar
cream
salt and pepper
½pt milk
1 tbsp butter
1 tbsp flour

Purée the mushrooms, sugar and onion with the stock in a blender. Heat it gently for 15 minutes, without letting it boil. Make a roux by pasting the flour into melted butter and stirring in the milk. Allow it to boil for 1 minute, then pour in the mushroom mixture. To reheat, bring back to the bubble but, again, do not let it rise in a boil. Remember to reserve two mushrooms and cut them into matchstick strips like mousetails. Just before serving, swirl 2 tbsp cream into the soup and scatter the mousetail strips on the surface.

Herb Bread

1 small crusty loaf
1 tbsp butter
½ tsp thyme
1 tsp tarragon

Rub the herbs in your fingers until they are powder, then cream them into the butter with a fork. Cut the bread as if to slice it but do not cut right through. Leave the bottom crust and about ½in of crumb unsliced. Spread the butter between each slice, press the loaf back together, wrap it carefully in foil and bake in the oven for 30 minutes at 200°C (400°F) Mark 6. Serve in the foil, unwrapping it at the table.

Golden Quarrels

So-called because of the noisy embrace of boiling oil and cold batter. Ideally these should be cooked on the table in a fondue cauldron, but be sure the oil is hot enough by dropping spots of batter in and seeing them hiss and move around.

3oz plain sifted flour
1 egg, beaten
1 tbsp Sajoer Lodeh paste
water
1/4lb firm mushrooms
2 celery sticks
cauliflower florets or
1/2 green pepper
2 tsp salt and black pepper

Mix the beaten egg into the flour with enough water to make a thick custard consistency. Beat in the paste (available from Indonesian shops) and the salt and pepper very thoroughly. Heat oil about 2in deep in a pan or fondue pot. Coat all the vegetables liberally in the batter and fry them in the oil until they are golden. Eat immediately.

Small Pies

These are individual pies to bake in small soufflé dishes and eat as an intermezzo between courses. Alternatively, with the ingredients multiplied, they could be an entrée. Buy frozen puff pastry.

4oz sliced ham
2oz spinach purée
2oz grated cheese
black pepper
1 tbsp chopped onion
2 tbsp butter
1/4 tsp nutmeg
yolk of an egg, beaten

Fry the onion lightly in the butter and remove it from the heat. Mix in the spinach and spices. Fill the soufflé dishes with layers of this, the ham and the cheese. Roll out pastry and cut a piecrust for each dish. Bake in the oven for 35 minutes at 200°C (400°F) Mark 6, having brushed the pastry with the beaten egg yolk. A different filling:

2oz minced veal
2oz ham slices
2 tbsp butter
2 tbsp chopped onion
1/4 tsp mace
2 tbsp spinach purée
1 egg, beaten
pinch salt and pepper
1 tsp French mustard
yolk of an egg, beaten

Fry onion in butter, add the veal and cook until brown. Mix in mustard, mace and seasoning. Beat spinach into the egg. Pack the soufflé dishes with alternate spoonfuls of each mixture and the ham. Make a piecrust, glaze with the egg yolk and bake as before. Experiment with your own fillings.

A variation on the sausage roll belongs to this genus of delights. Just wrap 1 slice cheese, 1 tbsp liver paté, 1/4 tsp nutmeg and 1/4 tsp black pepper tightly in rolled puff pastry. Seal the edges and bake in an oven for 35 minutes at 200°C (400°F) Mark 6.

Dragon's Tail

A traditional dish from the banquets of fantasy. According to rumour, many princesses were grateful to the itinerant chefs who slaughtered, butchered and cooked dragon.

1lb rolled shoulder of lamb	2 tsp salt
5 tbsp puréed spinach	1 heaped tsp rosemary
1 large onion, chopped	1 tsp black pepper
2 slices brown bread	sliced parsnips
1 tbsp butter	butcher's string

Cut the string on the rolled lamb. If it's stuffed, remove the stuffing. Unroll the lamb. Fry the onion in 1 tbsp of butter until it is dark brown. Mix it with the spinach purée (frozen spinach through a blender), the brown bread (crusts removed and crumbled finely) and the spices. Lay the mixture over the lamb and roll it up like a Swiss roll. Tie with string and roast in an oven for 1 1/2 hours at 200°C (400°F) Mark 6. Put a knob of butter and some sliced parsnips in the baking pan.

Prepare the following garnish:

1oz red pepper, chopped	4 or 5 stuffed olives, chopped

or any other colourful vegetable. Scatter them over the meat before you serve it, the way jewels used to encrust a dragon's belly. Serve the following medieval sauce called galantine:

crusts of 2 slices of brown bread	1/3 tsp powdered ginger
1/2pt chicken stock	1/3 tsp cinnamon
no more than a pinch of salt	2 tbsp wine vinegar
1 tsp galingale (Laos powder)	

Grate the bread and put it with everything else in a saucepan and simmer for 10 minutes.

Roast Pheasant

Much of the joy of pheasant comes from its traditional accompaniments of 'sand' and crisps, bread sauce and gravy.

2 young pheasants	1 tbsp butter
6 rashers streaky bacon	1/2pt mug dry breadcrumbs

Smear the breasts of the birds with butter and plaster the bacon over them. Wrap each bird in foil and bake on their sides for 45 minutes at 200°C (400°F) Mark 6. Remove the tin foil, replace the birds breast-upwards in the pan and put the breadcrumbs beside them. Return to the oven for 10 minutes. Since the juices from roasting have been appropriated by the breadcrumbs you are morally free to make a gravy in advance. Melt 1 tbsp butter in a pan and stir in 2 tbsp cornflour. Stir in ½pt water, 1 tbsp Worcestershire sauce, salt and pepper and ½ tsp tarragon. Simmer for 5 minutes. Heat potato crisps for the last 10 minutes in the oven.

Spicey Rabbit

On the rare occasions a wandering minstrel actually wandered, he might have been amazed by the flavour of this pot roast, scenting it through the forest, the evening meal of a lapivorous ogre and the beautiful damozel imprisoned in a tower of his croft.

3 plump pieces of rabbit
4 tbsp oil
1½ onions, chopped
1 tsp powdered garlic
salt to taste
½ tsp turmeric
½ tsp galingale
½ tsp ground cinnamon
water to cover
4 rashers streaky bacon

In a heavy casserole brown the rabbit in the oil. Add the onion and garlic and brown them. Add the salt and spices and fry for 5 minutes on a low heat. Pour in the water and bring back to the boil. Remove from heat. Lay the bacon over the islands of rabbit and bake for 1 hour in an oven at 240°C (475°F) Mark 9. The liquid should have evaporated into a paste. Serve with baked potatoes.

Fish in Weeds

1 large mackerel
1 lettuce
¼pt wine vinegar
¼pt water
3 tbsp butter
salt and pepper
1 tbsp lemon juice
1 tsp garlic powder
¼lb broken almonds
2 tsp tarragon
2 leeks, cut in strips

Clean the fish, remove gills, but leave the head on. Boil a big pot of water and immerse the fish in it for 10 seconds. Carefully peel off its fins and skin, except from around the head and tail. Wilt the lettuce in the same bubbling water for 1 minute. Spread out the lettuce leaves and lay the fish on top. Mash the garlic, tarragon, almonds and lemon juice into 2 tbsp butter with salt and pepper, and smear this into the fish's pouch. Wilt the leeks in the good old boiling water and lay them along the bottom of a long narrow ovenproof dish. Wrap the lettuce round the fish and lay it on top of the leeks. Leave the head and tail poking out of the lettuce. Sprinkle salt and pepper over all, pour on the liquids and put the rest of the butter on the lettuce. Cover dish with foil and bake for 30 minutes in an oven at 220°C (425°F) Mark 7. Serve it in a little of the liquor, festooned with weeds (leeks).

Roe Broth

The best way to eat venison, be it roe deer or any other. You may have to order it from a butcher so ask for the cheaper meat from the shoulder.

1½lb venison
1 walnut-sized piece of ginger
1 bottle red wine
1 large onion, chopped
1 tsp ground mace
½ tsp marjoram
salt and pepper
1 tbsp butter

Cut the venison up into small cubes and trim off fat. Peel and grate the ginger. Mix everything except the butter together and soak the meat in this marinade for 24 hours. Remove the meat but keep the marinade. Fry the meat in the butter until it is a little brown, put it and the marinade into a casserole, cover it and put it in the oven for 1½ hours at 200°C (400°F) Mark 6. Check it every 30 minutes, adding a little water if it starts to dry out and testing the seasoning.

Rosee

If ever a dessert brought forth life this one did.

1 plum
1 ripe pear
½pt double cream
3 tsp brown sugar
¼ tsp powdered cinnamon
3 drops rose essence

Liquidise the peeled and cored pear and the stoned plum with the sugar and cinnamon, moistening with a little of the cream if necessary. Whip the cream until it forms peaks and fold it into the fruit thoroughly. Now add two drops of rose essence and taste. The rose flavour should be subtle so that it is present but hard to diagnose. You might need one more drop. Serve it in two delicate liqueur glasses and lay a sheet of edible silver foil (called Vark and available from most Indian stores) over the top. Lay one rose petal on each.

Gilded Gingerbread

Half-way between a bread and a biscuit, this is the sort of gingerbread that men are made of.

¼lb of flour plus 1oz
1 tsp baking powder
¼ tsp salt
1 walnut-sized knob of ginger
1½ tbsp butter
1½oz soft brown sugar
¼pt golden syrup
½ egg, beaten

Mix 1/4lb flour, baking powder, salt and the ginger, peeled and grated very finely, in a bowl. Cream the butter, sugar, syrup and egg together then add them to the dry ingredients, mixing well into a dough. Add a little more flour if it is too sticky. Roll the dough out on a floured surface or pat it flat with your hands. Cut out shapes like the lady's initials, slender leaves or love knots, put them on a sheet of greaseproof paper in a baking tin and bake for 15-20 minutes, depending on the thickness of the dough, in a pre-heated oven at 190°C (375°F) Mark 5. Gild them while they are still hot by laying sheets of edible gold or silver (sometimes called Vark and available from Indian emporia) on each biscuit.

Salad Days

Vegetables have no fear of death. Their serene pantheism leads them to see being eaten as a mere change of shape and not an end. The thin, sweet, priestly water that slides through a plant's capillaries is too refined to serve as blood, as a stream of corpuscles swollen with a sense of self, and yet each vegetable has an identity, and their personalities must be studied to complement their neighbours at the dinner table. There are a million ways of silencing a carrot's rustic chatter, but as an accompanying dish, try taking advantage of the true nature of plants. Here, then, are a few methods for serving vegetables as themselves. Always buy fresh ones (with a few exceptions) and cook them immediately before you eat.

Asparagus: Peel stems, remove tiny leaves from tip. Place in boiling, salted water for 20 minutes. Serve with melted butter, salt and pepper.

Aubergines: Slice aubergines and soak for 1 hour in water. Dry them, coat in flour, sprinkle with salt and fry in hot oil until brown.

Beetroot: Peel, cut into thick slices, place in boiling water for 30 minutes. Drain water. Put spoonful of butter, salt and pepper into pan and toss beetroot until butter melts.

Broad Beans: Shell fresh broad beans. Boil until tender (20 minutes—or less). Serve in white sauce.

Broccoli: Boil broccoli for 10 minutes. Serve with melted butter, salt and pepper.

Brussel Sprouts: Peel off damaged leaves, cut back stalk. Boil for 7 minutes. Drain water and treat as beetroot.

Brussel Tops: Wash and remove damaged leaves. For ½lb tops, boil 1in water and put in the tops. Cook for 10 minutes, stirring. Drain and treat as beetroot.

Cabbage: Remove damaged leaves. Cut roughly and boil in water and 2 tbsp wine vinegar for 10 minutes. Drain and treat as beetroot.

Carrots: Top and tail, scrape, slice. Boil for 15 minutes. Treat as beetroot.

Cauliflower: Wash, trim stalk to lowest florets. Boil whole for 15 minutes. Pour on melted butter, salt and pepper.

Celery: Make a *blanc* by pasting 1oz flour in 1 tbsp melted butter and beating in 2pt water, juice of 1 lemon and 1 tsp salt. When it's boiling, add the trimmed celery and cook for 15 minutes.

Chinese Lettuce: Cook as celery, but add 2 tbsp soya sauce to the *blanc* before you serve.

Courgettes: Wash, top and tail, slice and boil for 3 minutes. Treat as beetroot.
Garlic: Gingerly peel each clove and boil in salted water for 30 minutes. Drain and butter as beetroot.
Leeks: Cut off beard and dry leaves. Split in two, wash well. Boil in salted water for 12 minutes. Drain and treat as beetroot.
Mange-tout: Trim and boil for 10 minutes. Drain and treat as beetroot.
Mushrooms: Wash but do not peel. Bake, put under grill, fry in butter or boil for 5 minutes and treat as beetroot.
Onions: Top and tail, peel. Bake and serve with melted butter, salt and pepper.
Parsnips: Top, tail and scrape. Cut into fingers and bake in same pan as a roast until a little burnt, or boil for 15 minutes and treat as beetroot.
Peas: Use frozen peas. Do not thaw. Empty packet into 1in boiling water and return to boil. Drain and treat as beetroot.
Peppers: Hull them, cut into rings and sauté in butter, salt and pepper for 10 minutes.
Potatoes: 1 of a 1000 ways: peel and slice potatoes and 2 leeks. Put in a casserole with 1/4pt milk, lots of salt and pepper and 2 tbsp butter. Bake for 1 hour in an oven at 200°C (400°F) Mark 6.
Red Cabbage: see Kraut (p. 22).
Spinach: Remove damaged leaves. Chop roughly and put in pan with 1in boiling water. Stew for 10 minutes. Drain and treat as beetroot.
Spinach Roots: Hard to find; worth it. Clean thoroughly and boil for 15 minutes. Remove and peel. Return to fresh boiling water for 10 minutes. Drain and treat as beetroot.
Spring Greens: Cook like brussel tops.
Swedes: Peel, chop and boil until soft (15 minutes). Drain and mash with 2 tbsp milk, 1 tbsp butter (or more), salt and pepper.
Sweet Potatoes: Peel, slice and boil for 10 minutes. Remove to a dish with 2 tbsp milk, 1 tsp salt and 1 tbsp brown sugar. Bake in oven for 20 minutes at 200°C (400°F) Mark 6.

Baked: Scrub one medium-sized potato for each person and bake in a hot oven like an ordinary potato for about 45 minutes or until they are soft. Split and serve with butter.

Fried: Peel and slice the potatoes and sauté them in butter, sprinkling with a little brown sugar and pepper.
Tomatoes: Bake whole, or grill, salted. Stew, peeled, for 5 minutes with salt, 1 tsp sugar and 1 tbsp vinegar.

The Morning After

Great thoughts are born within the minds of men during that hour when the shape of the window looms less blackly and the sparrow relieves the nightingale of the relay-baton of song. The failed seducer is asleep however, having finished off the wine after running his guest home, and the issues jousting in the mind of the successful Lothario might well be more practical than metaphysical.

Assuming he was able to maintain his disguise throughout the evening he must now ask himself whether he has the energy and inventiveness to persist in the deception. Ideally he could gently wake her, explain that he was having her on and apologise; she would admit that she was not a beautiful and gullible student but a millionairess looking for a deceitful chef and they would both live happily ever after. An unlikely scenario; honesty may be the best policy but an explanation seems unthinkably traumatic in the hellish light of dawn.

Whatever he decides to do, whether talk about it, let it drift on for a week or two, relying on her to end it, or propose marriage, the first steps are the same: at a suitable hour slip silently from the room, wash, shave and clean your teeth. Prepare breakfast in bed for you both and wake her with it—not by balancing the tray upon her slumbering form (the sight of a counterpane smeared with Eggs Benedict is no way to start the day), but by the method Marguerite's maid used in *Camille,* lightly spraying perfume into the air two feet above her head.

It might be now that she will stare at you for a while, frowning in a puzzled sort of way, and remark that you are not the same as you were last night. Do not fall to your knees begging forgiveness (unless your experience to date suggests that this sort of behaviour will interest her) and do not try to be witty. No one is witty first thing in the morning. Instead appear incredulous: last night? I remember nothing of last night except you . . .

There are ways to end an affair there and then should you want to. The cad will have a hundred lies up his dressing-gown sleeve for why he can never see her again, the coward will say nothing but answer the phone in a foreign accent when she calls and avoid any place where she might be. Such devices are for the closet misogynist and beyond the scope of this little book. The problem for the true lover is what to do next. Did he, in an unguarded moment, promise

to take her with him to Machismos and raise bearded children in the sun? Must he live forever with a second-hand Buddha, and how will he explain it to the landlord?

Staying in character, the stiff Manhattan will allow her twenty minutes to dress then bundle her into a cab with a promise to call her; the Bohemian will vanish after breakfast leaving a note and the hippy's house will be suddenly invaded by a folk group or his weekly yoga class. There are limits to any impersonation.

The only really sound advice is to play it by ear. More than likely, your guest will have changed from being a receptive acolyte into a woman with a fairly firm vision of the future, if not a lunch appointment with someone else. Anyway, the next ball is usually in her court.

Occasionally, however, the unforeseen will happen. A silence will permeate the room like the smell of distant curry. Your beloved will make no effort to prompt a plan of action, will formulate no decisions, only look at you to learn what happens now. Seize the opportunity! Resort to the final, marvellous solution and stop seeing the disguise as a disguise and nothing more. Become your alter-ego. After all, it was only custom that dictated your way of life up until last night, and there is nothing sacred about habit. Living on a Greek island or in New York may well turn out to be enormous fun, and the Latin Quarter is a spicier slice of life than the Anglo-Saxon. Troubadours enjoy the benefit of a leisurely climate, cheap Châteauneuf du Pape and the best bouillabaise in the world. So start to laugh, give the lady a kiss, leave your job, sell your flat and move to medieval France.

Raw Aurora

Trying to ignore the wine-dark circles under your eyes, prepare the following breakfast: a tiny cup of Greek coffee, a glass of water, plain yoghurt and honey and fresh sardines.

Greek Coffee

Ask at a grocer's for Greek or Turkish coffee. It is ground exceedingly small. Unless you have *brikia,* use a small saucepan into which you put 2 coffee cups of cold water, 2 tsp coffee and 2 tsp sugar. Stir once and bring it slowly to the boil. Remove from the heat and stir once more, then bring it back to the boil. Pour it into the cups.

Sardines

12 fresh sardines
4 tbsp olive oil
1oz plain flour
salt and pepper

Heat the oil in a frying pan until it sizzles. Holding each sardine by the tail, roll them completely in the flour, heads and insides and all. Fry them until they are crispy, turning only once. Sprinkle with salt and pepper and squeeze a lemon over them. Offer fresh bread and butter. An old loaf can be rejuvenated by moistening the crust and putting it in a warm oven for a while.

The Bohemian Matin Call

The few people left in this world who actually try to live in the old Bohemian way, wan academics mostly, drifting through their third degree at our older universities, seem to alternate their breakfast habits between the full fry-up and just black coffee, with no half measures. The larger option, however, is indulged in roadside cafés and is usually a preliminary to going to bed rather than its reward. The plate is piled high with fried bread, tomatoes, bacon, sausages, eggs, mushrooms and fried slices of black pudding, washed down with Camp coffee or brackish tea.

A more civilised idea might be croissant, a gift from the old baker who likes to patronise the arts, and good, genuine, coffee. Or there is always the omelette . . .

Omelette Bohème

4 eggs
2 tbsp water
1 tbsp butter
salt and pepper

Separate the eggs. Beat the yolks with the water, salt and pepper; beat the whites into a froth. Fold white into yolk. Heat the butter in a clean pan over a very hot flame. Pour in half the egg and immediately stir it with a fork. Roll the liquid egg to fill the pan. Leave for 2 minutes then fold in two. Eat at once.

Early to Bed, Early to Rice

It is never easy to cook breakfast when last night's washing-up is hanging around in the kitchen, but it is worth it for a good kedgeree. Make it the day before and heat it well in the oven while you are frying a couple of spicy butcher's sausages and preparing toast and a big pot of Indian tea. Include on the tray English mustard in a silver pot, marmalade and two small glasses of orange juice or one of the more exotic fruit nectars.

Kedgeree

1lb smoked haddock fillets
½pt mug dry rice
milk
2 hard-boiled eggs, chopped
3 tbsp cream
2 tsp French mustard
salt and black pepper
chopped parsley

Boil rice, drain and wash in boiling water. Poach the fish by covering it in milk in a shallow pan and simmering for 20 minutes. Taste the fish liquor. If it is not too salty use it (otherwise use an equal amount of milk) to mix with the fish, rice, chopped eggs, mustard, cream, parsley, salt and pepper. Garnish with a little red pepper. Kedgeree should be moist, so reheat it in a very hot oven with a lid on it.

Breaking Fast

Oranges, once golden Hesperidean worlds of nectar and delicate, fragile flesh, have become, in the sticky hands of rucksack wayfarers on trains, a fruit to be shunned. Not by the child of the Light. The hippy starts the day with one, peeled and pithed, attracted by the sacred colour and tongue-fur cutting acidity. Similarly, he devours quarts of jammy liquid in the name of yoghurt and sacks of laxative husks in pursuit of several elusive and probably harmful vitamins. Time was when a fragrant cigarette and a Janis Joplin track would do.

For your guest then, bring on plain yoghurt and honey, a bowl of nuts, the aforementioned orange and, to drink, apple juice, heated without letting it boil with a cinnamon stick floating in each glass. The scientifically minded suck the liquor through the stick. Sometimes even they pig out on pancakes.

Index